WOLF MOON BLOOD MOON

Wolf Moon Blood Moon

poems ED FALCO

LOUISIANA STATE UNIVERSITY PRESS

BATON ROUGE

Published by Louisiana State University Press

Copyright © 2017 by Ed Falco

All rights reserved

Manufactured in the United States of America

LSU Press Paperback Original

First printing

DESIGNER: Michelle A. Neustrom

TYPEFACE: Sina Nova

Poems in this collection appeared previously as follows: "While Falling to Sleep," *Blackbird;*
"The Burned Boy" and "Wish," *Copper Nickle;* "Port Authority Story," *First Circle;* "At the
Beginning of Marriage," *Literary Review;* "Faith" and "March 20, 2003," *Mississippi Review;*
"After, Climbing Dragon's Tooth," "April 10, 1988," and "Tsunami, East Japan," *Prairie Schooner;*
"Disembogue," "Dust," "Essay: On Language," "Essay: On Love," "Koi," "Meditation on Loss,"
"Quantum Theory," and "Wolf Moon," *Southern Review;* "Black Gift," *VIA: Voices in Italian
Americana;* and "Framed Picture on a Writing Desk," *Zone 3.* "Meditation on Loss" was awarded
the *Southern Review*'s Robert Penn Warren Prize in Poetry.

Library of Congress Cataloging-in-Publication Data are available from the Library of Congress.

ISBN 978-0-8071-6718-2 (pbk.: alk. paper) — ISBN 978-0-8071-6719-9 (pdf) —
ISBN 978-0-8071-6720-5 (epub)

What falls away is always. And is near.

—Theodore Roethke, "The Waking"

Contents

Meditation on Loss

Koi

A blue heron dips its beak into the backyard pond and lifts from beneath dark water a foot-long koi, the white one with bright red like an ink spill between its eyes, back to the dorsal fin.

Her husband built the pond with slate and cement, added at her wish a waterfall. Recirculated water trickles down stones and drops into the pool. There were goldfish in it then, scores of them breaking the surface when she dropped the flaked food in.

She thought the koi looked bloodstained and said so before her son slipped it into the pool, knelt at her feet in front of the wheelchair, rested his head a moment in her lap. He said, "It's all right, Mom," in a voice so like his father's that she managed to lift a gnarled hand and rest it on his gray hair. It was almost as if he were a boy again come to her with a skinned knee or a child's small heartbreak to be stroked and comforted. She tried to say again that the koi's red stain looked like blood and again he said, "It's all right, Mom," before he called for his sister, who came out of the house and into the sunlight carrying a tray of medicines.

The heron tilts its beak up to secure the koi, which is curiously still.

Forty-five years in the same house so that everywhere she looks she sees him: on his knees with a trowel smoothing the freshly poured cement of the patio; shirtless in the yard, a shovel in his grimed hands, digging this or that, always digging something. She sees him in the plants and flowers, especially in the plants and flowers, in the bleeding hearts and salvia, in the crowded hostas and the clustering hen and chicks, in the showy pink hibiscus, which shouldn't grow here but do and come back year after year, their roots deep under the foundation where they huddle in a pocket of warmth. All those years, home from eight hours in the shop and then out in the yard, digging in the garden, planting something new, working on this or that project while she tended the kids, before the kids were all grown and she tended only him.

Today she's sitting in the sun, her daughter in the house, on the phone. She wants to speak, but she long ago lost words. Her body has shriveled and crumpled into itself. The heron's great wings open in a magnificent show of blue. It rises into the air carrying in its beak the bloodstained koi. She watches as long as she can, and feels herself growing smaller as the blue of the bird is swallowed by the blue of the sky, till for an instant it's only that ink-spill bloodstain that remains, the bright speck of it on the air, a momentary spark or a flame about to disappear.

After a Neighbor's Death by Fire

The spiny burr that protects a chestnut's fruit
    Green needle-sharp slivers split in quarters
Litter the roadside after an overnight fire:
    Shadows sway to the flames' rowdy music

Windows explode clapboard crackles as it burns
    And my neighbor the one who might or might not nod
In response to my greetings inside wreathed in smoke
    His weathered body drifting into night.

This morning a light rain slicks the road as I walk past rubble:
    Crows cackle from the chestnut's heights
A pair of goldfinches dart through leaves, a woodpecker
    Somewhere drumming on a tree, and the creek

The one that follows the bottom of a nearby deep ravine
    Runs as it always does, a constant trickle
Burnishing pebbles that sparkle in its silt.

On My Mother's Ninety-fourth Birthday

My older brother leans forward in his chair to talk to our mother. He throws his hands about as he speaks, attentive, concerned, inquiring about her health. I can see how he struggles to resume his place as caretaker, as a man in control of his own affairs and others—his former self, the one before he woke up lost, his life scattered as a jigsaw puzzle flung across a strange room. He gesticulates. He works hard to be convincing, as if auditioning for a difficult role.

Our mother worries about him. She can no longer walk more than a few steps and everything she does she does in pain. She frets over him, her first-born. He's not taking his medications as prescribed. He's not eating right. She gesticulates, too, as well as she can manage. She implores him to take care of himself and her arms fly up from the arms of her wheelchair.

They lean close to each other, their eyes on each other's eyes, mother and son, boy and young woman, lost in the moment and searching for each other somewhere along the long corridor of years.

Morning Voices

This morning's raucous quiet: din of a lawnmower
    Pulse-like swell of cicadas chattering in the brush
        Trucks grumbling along a nearby highway.

Under a sea of high thin clouds, a sheer ocean of sky
    The dead are islands: an archipelago
        Of mute echoes, of resonant silence

Their voices still within this gorgeous commotion—
    Crow call, water burbling, wind rough in trees—
In a weed's play, against skin, in the heart's vibrations.

Under the racket of this day's distractions
    Under the birds' clamorous singing
        Under lapping waves of noise

Their stopped tongues their stilled voices speaking.

Disembogue

Disembogue: to flow out or empty, as the spirit
Disembogues into air earth water fire upon death
The body upon transubstantiation to discharge
By pouring forth as a river disembogues into the ocean.

Spirit the soul hovers in green in crimson while vultures
Perch in the limbs of a dying tree eyeing what passes below:
On my evening walk the hour crepuscular their heads
Cocked in my direction as light disembogues into darkness.

Overhead a whippoorwill its three peaking notes repeating
Two crows call to each other a squirrel rattles dry leaves
On the nearby highway a semi roars through its gears
Before dark arises and sound disembogues into silence.

Green the lively commotion the swelling erupting entry, spills
Scatters as leaves fall as the boulder disembogues into the shore.

Meditation on Loss

One moment of meditation leads to sailing down stairs. First there's the consideration of loss: Though she has metamorphosed into the young woman I love, the child I love is no longer here. Her hand wrapped around my two fingers as we walked along a beach, she turned light into water: Look! Look! The sun is like a waterfall! Sunlight spilled to the ocean through a break in thick clouds. Such is the jolt of that memory I have to stop a moment till it weakens, because I miss her and the years are falling away. I'm on a city street. Manhattan. Midday. Summer. I'm sitting on a brownstone stoop with my hands over my eyes, and it's in that willed dark that the basement door opens and I start down stairs. Now I'm a child. That's my mother in our Brooklyn home, in the basement where I'm not allowed to go. She's putting a penny in the fuse box. The lights are out. I remember the darkness. I watch her from the top of the stairs as she pushes in the penny where the fuse is supposed to go and then the blue flash, bright solid blue like a lightning strike might look deep underwater, and then for a second her hand is on fire. She flies away from me through the dark, lit up by a flame that envelops her hand before it's dark again and I'm sailing down the stairs because the memory is partly what happened and partly the dream of it that recurred for many years. My mother's hand is on fire and then it's not and she's holding me in the dark. How strange is this world? My mother's flaming hand, the waterfall of the sun. The way the years flash past, and a moment never ends.

After, Climbing Dragon's Tooth

All that week and for a long time after, nothing was the same: the wind on Dragon's Tooth, sunlight over the valley, a young woman who asked if I knew the name of a kind of tree. Late afternoon sunlight, wind bullying treetops along the ridge. She was in her early twenties, dressed in jeans and a T, with white and red and bright green in her sneakers. One girl climbing on the way up—this was a popular trail and the spring day drew us out, mostly from the college, everyone's from the college around here—one girl wore a VT cap with a maroon and black ribbon pinned on the brim.

I had read that after a great trauma part of the mind remains for many months locked in rethinking, and I imagined a room-sized computer programmed to answer the question "Why is there suffering in the world?" Look at us on this budding-green mountain, hustling up rocks for a look out over the long valley. We stop and bow to wildflowers along the trail. We stretch out on boulders in homage to the sun. We offer praise with every effort of foot on rock, climbing only to be climbing.

At the top, on the ridge, I sit on a jagged outcropping of rocks and share a snack with my companion. We drink from the same bottle of water and are quiet. Her hand slips over mine in the last of the sunlight—and where there should be love or joy or gratitude there's only sorrow, as if it's the only feeling left in the world. All that remains to do is look out from this jagged tooth of rock and listen to wind through crevices and in leaves, as if that sound, so other and unknowing, is this world's one true word.

The Leading

Storms all morning quick flashbulb flare of light
Thunder's husky growl I'm immersed in sleep

Outside roses, yellow and red daylilies
Stand up to the passing frenzy of wind and rain

Later in sunlight the ground soaked and spongy
On my way to collect the morning paper a raptor

Long-winged heavy lifts from my ivied chimney
All I catch is a glimpse of wings and air disturbed

And I'm back in a dismal moonless dream
Parched scabland a mildew earth-smell cave

A crow lifts its heavy body from a stump and flies away
I'm alive in two worlds this world's sun rain bright flower

The other world immanent a crow's a raptor's wings
In sleep in waking leading into that long dark waiting

March 20, 2003

That's a child missing limbs. I can't determine the sex. The body is small and burned as it floats down like a dark leaf, lazily, rocking, a black snowflake falling through a green forest. There's a war and it's snowing. Bulldozers level trees, the machine roar deafening. Jets fly past barely above the treetops. Hundreds of jets trailing flame. It's hard to believe they're piloted by humans but they are and not monsters but young men and women, most still near childhood just doing what they're told screaming jets over treetops.

Winter's coming on. The woods are filling up with black snow.

Tsunami, East Japan

The way water assaults the shore isn't an act of violence
Unless you're driving to work as the road darkens then ripples
The dull morning brain chugging toward comprehension.

Perhaps you say out loud, "That's water"
Before a house swirls over land
Taking point in a procession of cars, sheds, boats

Slowly— That's the thing, how slowly the sea moves
As if it means no harm, and surely it does not
Blue sky throughout the prefectures undisturbed by final prayers

Last violent struggles, cold shocks, roar and silence.
For now a shimmer of black water laps at your tires
As you make a three-point turn and drive off

Into all the days that will follow: morning sun setting
A seascape alight with its fire, salmon cloudscapes at night
The gathering waters still trailing behind you.

Dust

1

Motes of dust in barred sunlight.
Sunday afternoon, rooms full of cigarette smoke.
Upstairs bedroom, prelude of slammed doors.

Then, I'm just a child. Now
My daughter scurries in front of fear
She owns, calling who she knows

Can save her, and I reach over the bed
Hold her under quilts till she settles
Head burrowed to my chest where sleep comes

Guarded from creatures that can't climb this bed.

2

Soon the reasons you left will only be dust:
Dead rise from wounds nameless. Leaves stuck
To cerement, they wind dizzily out of cerecloth

Reverse the intricate weave wound in life
Stumbling from one friend to another, lover
To lover, each time bandaging wounds tighter

Till there's no air left, we've covered
Every feature and there's nothing left
But to go on spinning till we reach our dust.

3

The way morning mist kneels on water
Or crimson streaks of cloud at sunset.
Pearl ice drop suspended from a leaf.

Still, when silence settles and speech comes
It's always dust. For praise: heat that lives
At the body's center, white or chocolate

Skin of a woman's thigh. Eyes that see
A child in her red coat against a bank
Of snow. Words seem false to the purpose.

Born of dust they speak only of themselves:
Dressed in dark habits they stoop
Are self-conscious. As if the spine

Is twisted and they can't without
The most awful contortions look up.

4

There's a character around here, an older man
Who lets his beard grow long and shaggy.
At nightspots he shows up wearing earphones

Stands in front of the tallest speaker, sways
To loud music. He jerks when a chord strikes
Home and I'd like to write a poem of praise

For a man who allows himself such freedom
Music's lover and the way the body moves.
I open my mouth and out comes dust.

I make a man running from fear.
With no father to hold him in quilts
He draws up the warm cover of music

And lies down beside darkness.
What's true is not the issue.
This is the way I see the world:

Fear, the engine that drives us all.
Thirteen steps up a dark flight of stairs.
This is such a small matter, a childhood

Fear: frail limbs under cold sheets
Voices through the heating grate
A door slams something breaks someone falls.

5

So we're back again in childhood
Now we've made this child who is
No one special, who could walk outside

This moment where the temperature
Has dropped below zero and a cutting
Wind turns around the house. "I'm going

To Grandma's," she'd say and walk out
The door with her grown-up look
A delicate half-wave, carrying a

Yellow basket. She'd take our lives
With her surely as her own. This
A child's best gift: keys to the self's

Prison, though some refuse it and then
Their cells fill with a child's litter.
Your father, spent his salary on whores.

Your mother, leaves you at three locked
In a car while she drinks late at a local bar.
My father's black fists teach me cowardice.

This is the hateful love we share.
Solid as earth it pushed us together
Nights in front of a red brick hearth

In a snowy city: cars squeal on ice
Outside, sirens, foul-mouthed city kids
Drag sleds, fight, and we most of the time

Naked before the fire, full of sleep and talk.

6

These are memories now, fine as dust.
The particulars settle in an inner room
We think airless but takes its allotted space

On a landing perhaps off that flight of stairs
I never stop walking, waiting for an unfamiliar
Noise, counting steps through dark the years

Layer with loss and betrayal. You trusted me
And I rose from sleep to shut the closet doors
Or long mornings in bed, nights we walked through.

The way your body trembled as a child was pulled
From severed muscle and you clasped my hand.

7

Now you live across town and we live alone.
One night I dreamed we were still together
The next day I started this poem. Then

I thought I was writing about dust—strange
Since I wanted a love poem. But I've learned
To listen and not complain, and now I've kept it

Dust and all because it seems the only beauty
I can manage. It's early morning as I write
And outside my window the sun is bright on your garden:

Long stakes weathered and most toppled are wrapped
In the choking dead husks of vines. It's winter
And nothing grows while wind blows dirt along the ground.

April 10, 1988

Sun in black-and-white is white and the field beneath it is black, where I'm
standing with my brother, midday. That's the old farmhouse behind us. It's
red but not in this snapshot. In this snapshot it's black. Though not black,
really. A shade of gray. The red farmhouse is a lighter gray than our suit
jackets, which are almost black. A white carnation in the lapel of my jacket.
I'm being confirmed. This is my confirmation day, April 10th, 1988. I look like
I'm about eight though I'm probably older. My brother is in his mid-twenties
and women have always loved him, all women it seems to me now: our
mother, our aunts, both of our sisters, and in high school I was too young to
remember but I'm told all the girls. This is the year Vietnam begins to pull its
troops out of Kampuchea, and that country disappears, along with Pol Pot,
before it reappears as Cambodia, again, missing a couple million murdered.
This world, the year I'm confirmed, the sky is the lightest shade of gray and
it rushes on forever behind our black suits and the farmhouse and the fields.
The year our mother took a course in photography (thus the black-and-white
picture), a year before she moved in with her teacher and then married him
and lived a few miles away with a new family. My brother moved to San
Francisco before he moved back a few years later, when I was just starting
high school. He was sick. He moved back into his old bedroom and only
lasted a few months. At the funeral there were so many women crying it was
like a wave of tears breaking over fields that stretched out beyond the home
all the way to the farmhouse and this black-and-white picture which I hold in
my hand as I look at my brother, long gone, on the day I was confirmed, with
a white carnation pinned to my jacket.

Black Gift

There's a black box centered on my white quilt. A black box, a gift box, an expensive shirt came in, from an ex-lover / ex-wife to whom I am still married and whom I still love. It's a striped shirt, sea-blue, and it's hanging in my closet now and now there's a box in the center of my neatly made bed. What is the nature of daily life? Is it about work? It never feels that way, though I work hard. I work all the time. Life, though, feels like it's about something else and now here's this black box sitting on my white quilt like it means something. Life, the daily getting up and doing things and then going to bed, all the immense stuff that happens in that interval, the choking absence the surfeit of joy, life— What if we told children that love always leads to grief? Everything would change, I think. I know very little, but here's this black box in the center of my bed, and damn if it doesn't feel like it's speaking to me. Not just the box, not like it has a voice, but the whole scene: a neat bedroom, good furniture, a mahogany sleigh bed with a white quilt, morning light through the windows, and a black gift box centered on the white quilt. I don't know what it's saying but there's something about it being a gift box and it being black. It worries me—and so, of course, I thought I'd share it with you. A gift.

Jackson, Mississippi

On the descent into Jackson, the long aisle of our plane goes black. The dark is inside only a few seconds before it slips back out. We were all quiet in that instant the dark slipped in: fifty of us silent, listening.

For J.

You'd be old by now, had you made another choice.

I still think of you, not that we were ever close
Only someone who knew you well enough
To exchange a nod, a greeting, an amusing story.

I'm on board a plane flying over the Rockies
Emmylou Harris singing sweetly "See what you lost
When you left this world," and there you are

In a red blouse with that crazy unmanageable hair
A forced smile that could bloom into something real
As sunlight in a storm, flaring between dark clouds.

Your husband your daughter all your friends
They're laughing, making love, crying too
All the stuff we always do and have always done

But no one has forgotten you, J. You're like the shade
Under a dogwood on a summer day, a dark place
But beautiful, too: cool and somber, enticing—

And touched with just a hint of terror.

Ghost Bike

Wrapped in white tape, leaning against a utility pole
His bike looks spectral, a pale ride to nowhere
Or everywhere, surrounded by bouquets of bright flowers
Notes from friends and strangers taped to the frame:

A memorial to his passing, to his place of departure.
Overhead, a murmur of starlings swoops low, dissolves
Disappears in green crowns of trees that line the street
This street he started out on each morning, riding to class

Courting a future that came too fast.
Take this gift of flowers, this offering of notes and wishes:
Boy on a sleek bike peddling along a bright street, heading home.

Blood Moon

Memorials turn up everywhere on roadsides outside
Dorm rooms in front of movie theaters on the porch
Of a yellow clapboard house where a loaded gun
In the hand of a toddler in the hand of a twelve-year-old

A laid-off husband another's wife in the hand of a furious
A ghost so long alone a mind bound in shade in the hand
Of a heart gone to shale cracked and cold splintered
The eyes of an animal shining out of the dark.

Under a blood moon the memorials' bright flowers, shining.

Wolf Moon Blood Moon

On Your Way to the Theater

You're in a crowded restaurant on 7th and 45th
Grabbing a bite to eat before the show everyone's
Talking about—when you realize you're old.

Of course you know you're old. You'll be 70
So fast you can feel the G-forces distorting your cheeks,
But you used to be young. Really. Not that long ago.

Now you're eating a pear and almond-crusted
Goat cheese salad and you glance up to see everyone
Around you has thick heads of hair and bright

Eyes, excited to be here, midtown, most of them
On their way to see *The Lion King* or some musical
That will leave them singing their favorite songs.

You, though, you're on your way to see a play, the old-
Fashioned kind, where no one sings and everyone's
Dead or miserable by the end—and that thought brings

A laugh to your desiccated lips. What kind of world
Is this where everything moves so fast? Stars soaring
At unimaginable speeds and only the great darkness

Waiting. The flares of our spirits erupt in the night
To illuminate exactly nothing—except, maybe, each other.
Still, there's this delicious pear and almond-crusted

Goat cheese salad, which is good as it has to be because
Well, it is. And now you pay the check and you're off
To the theater and a play you've heard is disturbingly dark;

And, honestly, you hope they enjoy their enchanting songs.

In Answer to Your Question...

I'm a child playing alone in the dark
    on a rattrap staircase.
        The streets outside shimmer
with their common terrors.
    It's hot on the staircase
        and I'm playing with garden shears
slicing at air, jabbing at nothing
    a crab claw threatening shadows
        as I bounce down step after step
noises emerging, a monster growl
    a banshee shriek, a bark or serrated whistle
        the shears' blades making
their sizzling scythe slash sounds.

    The streets are the streets
        of mid-twentieth century Brooklyn
uneven slate sidewalks
    lines of side by side two-story homes.
        Who or what was it exactly
I was threatening? I'd have had no idea, I'm sure.
    Perhaps the monsters
        that turned up in my dreams
the gauze-wrapped lumbering creatures
    approaching my bed.
        Or the kids on the street
who made my childhood a long misery.
    But I'm pretty sure I wasn't thinking
        about any of that, just slashing
thrusting blades into the dark
    and cutting the air to pieces.

    Early in marriage you asked
why I threw stones at the river.

You said it was such a typically
          aggressive male thing to do
while I thought I was just throwing stones

     into the river.
               This is something I witnessed
          on the street in Brooklyn:
A boy taunted by an older boy
     hit him in the head with a bat
          a baseball bat, swung it like Ty Cobb.
The older boy wobbled
     suddenly a cartoon character
          his legs and arms rubbery
eyes spinning in circles out of focus
     before he dropped to the ground.
               And then there's the routine news
the daily atrocities, the bombs
     the stabbings the knives and semiautos
          the everyday bloodshed.

You asked why I pay so much attention
     to violence in the world, a long time ago
          before we split up.
     Here's my answer:
          Because I know what it is
to be a boy with garden shears
     hot in the muggy dark
          trying to cut the air's throat.

Port Authority Story

Before the city was beautified
For the good and dutiful
When pimps and whores
Owned the streets around 42nd
Where I took the bus from Port Authority
To college upstate New York
When I was seventeen
Fresh scrubbed from the suburbs
On my way back to school
Past the damaged the drugged the turned-out
A weather-beaten black man tall with greased hair slicked back
And a dun scar that ran from his crown
Over one dead eye down across his nose and lips to his chin
Swerved as he walked toward me about to walk past him
Stepped a little into my way
Just enough to slow me down
And as he passed ran the white palm of one big hand
Lovingly down the side of my face across my cheek
His fingers only reluctantly leaving my lips and chin
Before he continued on with a sigh
That I still remember forty years later
Talking with friends over drinks at a bar
Telling stories from our youth
Surprised at how vividly I recall that unexpected caress
As if I knew even then all that would pass
Passing between us in that touch

Regularly in My Dreams I'm Lost

Leaving Brooklyn on the L, a drunk sits beside me and wets his pants. I get off the train, and, here we go again, I don't know where I am. Is this Brooklyn? This isn't the neighborhood where I grew up so many years ago, where Bobby Somebody pushed my face into the hot tar of a summer street and I played kick-the-can on the corners. This is some other neighborhood and it doesn't look safe. Shit, there's someone following me. He's a guy maybe in his forties, which is how old I am now, and I'm running along shadowy streets and climbing a fire escape to an open window and when I get inside this tiny closet-size apartment the lights are out and someone's in here, someone's in the dark and I'm on the edge of screaming, which is how I awake, frightened, my heart blazing.

I can't tell you how many nights I've had dreams like this. Even in the good times, when we'd fall sleep on the old couch with the broken springs in front of the fire. Even then.

While Falling to Sleep

Man in a chair, balding, fat, whereas I'm buff, ripped, with long black hair.
Who is he? Girl at the mall in a black hoodie. On her, it looked like a cowl:
some kind of ancient priestess crone, her hands pressed together at her waist
as if in prayer. Where are the cats? I used to have two cats a long time ago
in a small house with you. Where are you, for that matter? This is our old
wide bed and I float around in it alone. The guy in the chair is getting to me.
I'm young and handsome but this guy's face, the guy in the chair, his face
is scarred with creases and crusty skin and rolls of fat along his neck. He's
disgusting. The girl in the hoodie walks toward me, I kneel at her feet. Really,
who is the guy in the chair and what is he doing in my bedroom with the
lovely painting of a sunset above my head?

It's cold outside. Frost blazes on moonlit fields.

At the Beginning of Marriage

I spent this day in a place of early losses
Reliving humiliation at the hand of my father.
We went to sleep back to back.

While our eyes were closed, moonlight
Came into the room.
I awoke suddenly and lighter.

Something dense had escaped my body.
My eyes opened to a changed world.
A white glow like mist, like fog lying in a hollow

Under moonlight settled around you.
Your skin mottled with bursts of pigment
Textured with tiny bumps and moles.

You were floating just under shallow water.
The ceiling fan turned and turned.
I rolled into your space and woke you.

I kissed the dark of your spine.
You turned and touched the front of your body to the front of mine.
That was like diving into warm water

The way you held me, the way your hands
Embraced and rocked and drew me toward heat.
Above us, on land, my father walked out of the room.

He closed the door gently behind him.

My Father as an Artist

He mostly copied the Renaissance masters' religious images
Though also bucolic scenes with streams and waterfalls.
He was in daily life a man furious with slights, injustices
The indignities of work below his intellect and talents.

The waterfalls he painted emerged out of another universe
One where he held a painter's palette, wore a smock and beret
Instead of the grease-smeared work clothes of a day laborer.
In the plaintive gaze of Botticelli's Madonna, a tranquil longing

An acceptance of suffering alive and captured in her eyes.
Paintbrush in his callused hand, transfixed before the canvas
Another being altogether, one rich with love and patience
Cast off cerements, pushed back a boulder, and arose from the grave.

This wounded man whose narrowed eyes taught me silence:
Father of rages, father of red fists and endless humiliation.

Wish

Catastrophes. Afflictions. Wish, a freshman in high school: stage lights of the future powering up, curtain rising, and he can't find his shoes and his pants are red and he has a pimple on his nose. He has to laugh. For instance, his flat hair. It's blond and thin and strings off his head to split around ears that pop out like fleshy satellite dishes beneath his temples. Class Cut-up. Least Likely to Succeed. He's been cursed by the god of genes to look like his ugly father, an unemployed house painter, mean drunk, Aloysius Millwright Sr., who proposes his fists will beat the screw-up into righteousness.

The day is a bully with his foot on Wish's neck. Out of his crowded trailer, through the squalid camp, along the rutted dirt road, to the crumbling asphalt that leads to the good road with the split-level houses that leads to Main Street where he walks three and a half miles to the high school preferring early rising and a long walk to being picked up by the bus at the trailer camp. Aloysius Millwright Jr. Wish. Most of his friends don't know where he lives, except Bax and Josh, because Bax has the money and Josh has the car and Wish has the connection. Together they drive over to Parrot, where the Pope lives, to score. The Pope, ex-biker turned God-fearer, believes weed is better than whiskey, likes to share a joint with the boys and talk of his days riding with the Pagans, turn each story of head-busting and whoring into a sermon which he ends with a stoned finger pointed at Wish's head as if to say Boy, are you listening?

Today Wish has a gun in his backpack. It's his father's, a Smith and Wesson .38, black, two-inch barrel. After school, he'll take the bus home with Bax, to his house with the deck that looks down over the valley, where he lives with his mother who's a professor at the college, where there are rooms full of books and magazines on the tables, where Josh and the others will meet them later, where they'll hang out in the basement and watch DVDs on the big-screen surrounded by speakers, where they'll sneak out to get high on grass Bax scored from his old babysitter; and then later, when they're all sleeping over, upstairs, in the living room, in sleeping bags on the white leather couches and wine-colored rug, he'll take it out in the darkness, in the soft light that fills up the room through long windows, he'll place it flat on the rug in that moonlight, a black jewel that will draw the boys to it. He can almost see them in his mind's eye, the boys sliding toward him as if pulled by a magnet, a black hole, dense center from which nothing escapes.

Gun in the palm of his hand in moonlight. Wish.

The Christmas Truce of 1914

For a few hours soldiers put away their guns.
    For one night and one morning
Exchanged gifts of cigarettes and dessert
    Retrieved bodies from no-man's land

Shook hands and sang familiar carols:
    For one afternoon and one evening
Someone brought out a soccer ball
    And they played like children home from school

Before they returned to the trenches
    And waited for morning and the savagery to come.

Framed Picture on a Writing Desk

When paper's a blank skin I understand
How nothing rides the wave of nothingness
White beach under the sun's pale-white caress
And if no wind blows hard across my hands
No spirit moves to touch or take my hand
My eyes turn there out of pure nervousness
There across the hall of years between us
To touch her image as a talisman.

She's one of hundreds on a crowded street
Locked out of a cinder block factory.
The picture was published without a date
But I can tell it's summer from the heat:
Her girlish face sweats across the century
Her eyes alive with bitterness and hate.

Terror in the Grass

—Schrik in het gras, from The Phillips Collection

A splotch of blood maybe on a patch of grass
Plus a hideous face black scarred burned and lashed.
Perhaps a fish nibbles on a rose rotted with blight.
Entrails hurled and smeared with globs of night
Like an innocent's garden appareled in celestial ash.

Atramentous

Atramentous: of or relating to ink, inky, black:
As night atramentous erases day, as light
Disembogues and dark emerges atramental and trees
And grass and houses, all the things of this world
Each in turn fade until what remains is sheathed
Voided, tenantless, a black surround, a scabland
As we scrabble and reach for purchase for a hold
In the atramental as searching in the atramentous
As night and night sounds and somewhere, a path.

The Burned Boy

Daisycutters. Josh is the smartest, whole crew. He reads *Newsweek* every week, cover to cover. He reads books on history on culture every political screed every polemic hits the stacks in Barnes and Noble, both sides of the issue. He's fourteen, youngest in the gang, skipped a grade. Daisycutters, he explains, don't explode on impact. They shoot out an aerosol spray on the way down then detonate above ground and a square mile or more goes up in flame. People trees buildings burn or blown up by the blast or the vacuum. Two tons of explosive power. You'd be like, man, if you were there? You'd be like boom, gone! Nothin' but atoms. So we dropped these like in Iraq? Oh yeah, and Afghanistan. The press here is all Where's the Iraqi Army? Where's the Republican Guard? Dude, like, we been droppin' daisycutters on them. Where do you think they are? They're in the wind, man. They're gone.

Sometimes at night Josh dreams war. He doesn't know what he thinks. He's against the war, like his father, but he doesn't know what he thinks. His head is full of pictures: bodies falling from the windows of the Twin Towers bodies on fire Iraqi children blown to pieces a boy with arms and one leg gone white cream smeared over his torso smiling for the camera as if he's happy. Josh's dreams: the torture chambers of Saddam Hussein, mass graves, the Kurds, that eerie picture of a woman dead sprawled out dead her skin covered with a patina of white powder and in her arms her baby an infant dead, white powder. He doesn't know what he thinks but he knows what he dreams, all these pictures. In his sleep. Where the armless boy rises and floats through fire to lie beside him in his bed, still smiling. It's almost like Josh is awake. He feels like he's awake. He sees the pale blue wall in front of him in moonlight. He feels the pillow he's clutching. His back turned to the boy with no arms and no leg whose charred torso is lathered in white cream. He wants to turn and speak to the boy, but he can't. It's like his body is locked in position. When he tries to speak the words won't come. He can think the words he can almost mouth them but all that comes out are little grunting sounds little moans. He tries to say Hello. He tries to say My name is Josh. He wants to say he's sorry for what's happened. He would like to comfort the boy if he could.

But he can't see him, the burned boy lying next to him in bed. The charred torso beside him on the sheets and Josh wants to ask him why he's smiling. But he can't speak. He doesn't have words. He wants to tell the boy that he'd help him if he could. But he can't speak. He tries in his dreams but the words won't come. He's asleep in his comfortable bed, in the suburbs of New York, the burned body of another boy silent alongside him.

The Travelers

That night on the deserted beach we shared bread and wine.
This was in Crete outside the village of Kolymbari off the Aegean.
I can't remember the details only that we talked until daylight.
Her name may have been Pia and I recall that she was German.
I came across her sitting on a rock with her feet in the water
In dying light in a breeze off the vast sea her blond hair cut short
A wicker basket beside her with a bottle of wine and a loaf of bread:
She held it out as if an offering and I laughed and sat beside her.

Nothing dramatic happened. I didn't fall in love. Nothing was revealed.
With our fingers we tore off chunks of bread, a crusty French boule.
When dark first lit the sea, we leaned against rocks and were quiet.
We didn't talk at first the bloody history of our countries—children
Gassed, crosses burned—we watched the sea and spindrift
And leaned against each other to ward off the night's cold.

Essay: On Language

The words we use to instill a sense of the ineffable
Carry us on a journey that's mysterious
As if your car makes a sudden left turn and accelerates
A child in the road leaps into her mother's embrace
A deer becomes a child and you hit the brakes
The panjandrum in the driver's seat this befuddled guy
At the wheel of an eighteen-wheeler hurtling down the road.

Language. He sat at the table, head in hands after work
A long day reminiscent of the day before and before
His child on the other side of the table watching him
A man given to gaucherie but driven by ambitions
A hard worker a laborer who came home at night
Greased in paint and sweat, soul tired and hungry.
He washed his arms and face and body with kerosene
Stripped to his underwear, rinsed off with a garden hose.
The boy watches him this brawny bare-chested man
Who looks up sees the child and asks "What the fuck
do you want?" Says "Get out of here before I beat your ass."

At night in Brooklyn the moon rises above two-family houses.
The boy stretches out on the roof and looks down to the street.
One evening a young woman a girl appears on a nearby rooftop.
She's barefoot in a white slip with long dark hair to her breasts.
In moonlight the slip is lucent and she hovers as an apparition
Her feet on the gutter, a gargoyle at her toes before she jumps.

Or falls. In the boy's memory she's there and then she isn't.
For the rest of his life he carries this moment with him.
When his father is dying from cancer (warning: don't wash
With kerosene) he places a hand on his chest to comfort him.
His father looks to the ceiling and says "Jesus, Joseph, and Mary!
They're coming for me!" before he takes a growling last breath.

The boy is an old man now and dreams this night of his own death.
He might prink all day getting ready for nothing or everything.
The girl on the rooftop his father at the table the moon and dying
All there on his tongue in every word he's ever spoken or put down
On paper or swallowed out of fear or fury. Each syllable a gesture
To the dark to the moonlight to that girl on the rooftop to his father
To the city to the angels coming for us all to the silence in between.

Essay: On Love

We were crossing a wide beach toward a blacktop parking lot.
I forget now who I was with or where we were going the year
The details of that particular beach vacation that summer break.
Morning not long after sunrise the day already hot.

In the parking lot six women wrestled a package of sorts
Emerged from the side door of an SUV onto the beach carrying
A small weight in a blanket like a sling or a makeshift stretcher.
Six women one at each corner of the blanket two at the middle.

I couldn't see what was in the blanket when they passed.
No one looked at us their expressions solemn touched by grief.
They stopped at the water's edge and a skeletal head rose up
Out of the blanket to look over the ocean as legs like sea straw

Fell gently to the gentle surf which washed over them.
To see the ocean one last time surrounded by friends.
August the Georgia coast sand dunes trees permanently twisted
Their crowns like long hair in a brisk endless wind blown back.

How many mornings have I walked barefoot along the beach?
Not enough. Never enough. Summer and heat and the ocean.
Dolphins threading waves terns pelicans gulls squawking

The salt smell of ocean and the shore stretching for miles
All the way back to the beginning and before as if the blue
Pool swelling out to the horizon licking wet at our feet is one
Body and the waves repeat a heartbeat that won't cease

Unlike our own which will. Dying woman at the water's edge
Carried by friends to be close one more time to the ocean
To sand under bare feet to the seashore on a summer morning.

Essay: On Gratitude

Hauling accumulated junk out of the garage on a summer day
The temperature in the 90s and sweat sliding into my eyes
Or the time pruning limbs from the backyard chestnut tree
I didn't see a hornets' nest the size of a basketball that fell
Unraveling a swarm that chased me my arms waving like a fool
Stung three times before I slammed closed the basement door
In the cool of that room cursed a ravaging assault of words
And then ice out of trays wrapped in a dish towel pressed
Wet and gelid over raw swelling the sting and burn of each bite

Soothed. Black dog sleeping in a sweep of morning sunlight.
Snow outside blown into blinding drifts after the night's storm
But now bright sun and bitter cold and the black dog asleep
In the kitchen while I'm in the living room by the fireplace
Feeding the lick of flames from a tumbling pyramid of cured wood.
A beautiful woman reaching on her toes to water the window plants.
She's asleep in the loft bed under a jumble of hand-me-down quilts
Her bare arm's dark skin blazing against the white of a quilt square.
In a little while I'll make breakfast, eggs bubbling in a black cast iron
Frying pan coffee perking on the back burner that rich aroma.
In our bed in our winter cabin I curl up next to the heat of her skin.

I came out of a raucous family the children of immigrants uneducated
Loud and brash who knew one thing above all, loyalty to each other
And yet fought among themselves like beasts breaking down doors
Screaming curses shouting political positions like weapon fire
Dozens of them huddled around a long dining room table the children
Scattered through the house and yard running chasing each other
Getting slapped across the face and screamed at or the belt might come off.
All that crazy chaos of aunts and uncles cousins and ancient ancestors
Year by year diminishes as the children are educated and move on
As the grandparents die and then the parents one by one till one day
It's only you and a few others and you're old and all there is is memory.

A cascade of bright sunlight through a hole in dark clouds. A beach
At dusk or sunrise. Your own family. A child's hand in your hand.
Winter and you're alone where it all started and you're not alone—
Every cursed and blessed every moment every syllable and touch.

Nor'wester

I woke to her touch beneath the covers
Tree limbs battering our torn-up rooftop.

I rose and swelled in the palm of her hand
Nuzzled in the swamp of our own heat.

The storm outside tearing the earth apart:
A kind of lover's music, a sonata.

Quantum Theory

That night your mother and I made love we didn't.
　　You were born and you weren't.
You joined the population of a parallel world
　　And you howled in your bedroom.
Years later I took a job in another state
　　And I turned it down. Your mother
Pursued a PhD in microbiology and stayed home.
　　She didn't fall in love with one of her students
Who didn't leave his young wife and move to Mexico
　　With you and your mom and his son.
We raised you together, grew more deeply bound.

Years passed and you too became a mother
　　And didn't, married a creep and a good man
Who abandoned you and adored you
　　Who had too much to drink, who drove
Home in the fog and crossed the double yellow
　　Who didn't hear the screams of a woman
In the oncoming car who was on the road and still in bed
　　Tucked in warm under quilts.
You visited him for years in jail and you grew old
　　Together in the comfort of your home.

In this world, darling, if you're listening,
　　Here's what I know:
That carnal night the stars were flaming
　　Your mother's touch burned through me
And you were a gift in the making.

Us

Then the wind came up while we were together in tall summer grass, the top of your head, that unruly wave of red hair, pressed into my chin. We had just finished together and were breathing hard. Wind whipped the tall grasses into a frenzy, while mountains rose up in a circle around us, our grassy meadow the bottom of a geological bowl. The air was cool against our skin and we fell apart, lay on our backs, looked up at the mountains, the sky full of fat white clouds drifting against an endless blue, wind, grass waving. We lay there like that holding hands, on our backs, beginning to feel the grit and dirt rubbed into our bodies but caught up mostly in the elements: the heat and sun and wind and that grass, the way the breeze came up as we were most urgent and rushed through the meadow and then the way we watched in silence, holding hands.

That's all that remains. This was more than fifty years ago and the names are gone as are the lies we must have told. But you, a you other than your name, which will come back to me in a moment, once the synapses click, and then will disappear again, you're still with me, the you that is your sweat-streaked body next to mine and that red unruly hair, the great curly mass of it, the two of us in that wind-swept meadow.

Forgive me, but I like you when you're sad ...

The way your face deepens and your eyes get so quiet air stops moving, all that busy signaling, a hundred billion messages, pictures, videos, cries for help or the fluctuations of the stock market—all of it comes to a stop in the quiet you create when you're sad.

You're young but your sadness is so ageless I can step into it and feel at home, as if I've just kicked off my shoes and settled into your skin. I know you when you're sad. Intimately. Like the slippery salt water on gray rocks at seaside when the sun hasn't been out for days and an icy rain falls in a mist. I'm comfortable there, as I'm comfortable with you.

All the plane flights and weather between us, all the distances and years, the kid with a cocked hat who pushed you under the bleachers, the people and places shouting this and that as they hurry along—all that slows and stills and then disappears when you're here.

I should say something funny to cheer you up, or wise to make it easier. You look confused. You're wondering what I must be thinking, and I understand. You're still too young to know there's nothing to say when the silence of this world gathers and drapes itself over you like a shawl.

Essay: On Ambition

On a beach rocks thick with algae and sea life at night
Crabs sand fleas sea snails moss distant lightning flashes
I sat contentedly with a friend and shared dreams.
This when I was an adult with a family of my own
After I was a worthless child stupid and ugly a little fool
My father's message emphasized with the back of his hand.
That was a long time ago and something I didn't talk about.
Neither did my friend raised with poverty and abandonment
Talk about his childhood; or for that matter my wife
Who lived through abuse that would bring an executioner to tears.
She was in the house that night taking care of the kids
While we sat out on the rocks my friend and I watching the ocean.

The boy who lived next door to me in Brooklyn where I grew up
Couldn't read which was something I didn't find out until years later.
We used to go to the library together on Saturday mornings
Where we'd each choose a novel return to our table and read
Or in his case pretend to read and it never occurred to me as strange
The way we'd talk about the characters in my story but never his.
He had a stack of pictures of his mother and father involved in group sex.
He flipped through them like a pack of playing cards dealt onto a table.
When he got in trouble for something he did in the hall with another boy
I was no longer allowed to see him and then he moved away.
I still think about him the way he spent hours turning pages
In books he couldn't read the black marks before his eyes a mystery.
I wonder what happened to him and where he is now and if he survived.

I got my undergrad degree at a state college and paid for it with loans.
My grad degree from a prestigious school far from Brooklyn and home.
On those rocks at night by the ocean the two of us and our dreams.
In the house behind us our wives and children the children playing
Our wives discussing the children and us and their dreams.
Under us in the black crevices in the cracks and seams and sand

Spiders and crabs and sea snails live out their natural lives.
Behind us an abandoned child nights without dinner a bruised son
Winters without heat a boy who can't read listening from the shadows
While we talk on and on willing to do whatever has to be done regardless.

Essay: On Courage

Oenomel: a drink made of wine mixed with honey, from the Greek
Oînos, meaning "wine" and *méli,* meaning "honey," which in English
Comes to mean anything that combines strength with sweetness
As my mother holds her oldest son's hand on the train back home
Traveling all the way to distant Brooklyn alone with her son
While her husband the only man she's known is off somewhere
With another woman. The details of the story don't matter.
Isn't it the oldest story in the world men betraying women?
That she's alone on the train with her son is what matters
That she met her husband for the first time when she was fourteen
And he was twenty in Brooklyn where they both were raised
He from a family dominated by men seven brothers
One tougher than the other and a mother tougher than them all
While she was from a family of five sisters and a working mother
Her father dead from tuberculosis while she was still a child.

She's on the train with her son on a bench seat holding his hand.
Her husband is in California with another woman. This is 1934
Deep in the grit of the Great Depression. She's alone on the train
With her four-year-old son the train clattering past mountains
On her way back to Brooklyn with a few dollars in her purse.
They went to California following a job for her husband.
She left when she found out about the other woman. Her son
Has no idea what's going on only the mountains sliding past
Which he'll remember all his life his hand in his mother's hand.

Many decades later when she's old her body finally betrays her
Though she answers every question about her health by saying "I'm fine."
This is long after the death of her husband who came home
And remained a tyrant but a tyrant in his place next to his wife
Their children five more before that part of life was over
Never knew about the other woman though the oldest son guessed—
What would make her leave her husband and return alone to Brooklyn?

This was all a long time ago in another era one not so great for women
And I wouldn't want the life she led to be the life my daughter leads.
A man I find myself now taking her not my father as a model.
She seemed to care only for others. She seemed to live
With the sole wish that others around her be safe and fulfilled.
When she died she died surrounded by great outpourings of love.

Essay: On Shame

What I remember about that night is that we didn't leave a tip.
We were so stupid drunk we sang "Ave Maria" all the way home
Under a teak black sky jitterbugging with stars bright as little moons.
This was me and my closest friend in the mountains upstate New York.
Those days we gambled, played pool, or hung out in strip clubs.
We drank all night and stuffed dollar bills under the dancers' garters.

What I remember is our waitress following us to the front door
Not the dancers strutting the stage as they stripped off their clothes
Not our conversation whatever it was that made us laugh like idiots.
We were both working menial jobs a couple of years out of college.
I spent my days chasing down loose horses on a breeding farm
Loading hay into barns mucking out stalls tending to the fences.
Her face was bright with anger we were too drunk to comprehend.

"Ave Maria" a tune we both knew from our days as good Catholic boys.
Oh Mary conceived without sin, pray for us, pray for us we sang and laughed
Like a couple of cartoon crows. One of the dancers was named Maria.
Only after the hangover a day or two later did I remember the waitress
How she sputtered about being stiffed after a night serving our drinks.
Not the dancers beautiful as they were peeling off sexy outfits
Not my close friend smart and witty who could always make me laugh
Not that raucous night and the long ride over a mountain under stars
But the waitress her eyes and driving home drunk singing "Ave Maria."

Faith

In the dark in the no-light at the field's center. Cows. Two cows. This is about what I believe. There are two cows in the center of a field that I cannot see. Two cows in the dark. I attribute my belief to a small part of the soul where knowledge resides and informs faith. That in the field there are two cows I cannot see. Not-cows which I cannot see. I know the cows are there because I know the owner of the field. He lives in town. He sold off the herd he said except two cows. These two cows. I know the cows are here because I can hear them. I hear them here making cow sounds which are mostly munching and chomping sounds. *Moo. Moo.* That's me. I say *Moo, Moo.* I don't know why. Sometimes I talk to myself. I tell myself to have faith. Here in the center of this dark field where I can't see a blessed thing, this seems like a good time. How did I get here? I don't know. I don't have the faintest idea. I wouldn't even swear that I'm here, it's so dark, except I hear the cows munching and I started out to cross the field. I was bored. That was before I got scared. Now I'm not bored. I'm scared because I can't see. I'm completely in the dark. It's exciting. I'm lost. Here I go. I'm walking toward what I'm sure are two cows. *Moo,* I say. So they know I'm coming.

Girl on the River

Beneath limestone cliffs pockmarked with caves
Girl in a red kayak navigates a slate blue river:
    Yellow paddles catch the sun
        Water shimmers as it spills
            Into the body of the river.

Where silt swirls around boulders, the river floor
    Drops in submerged pools
        Alligator gar hovering at the bottom
The moment silent but for the always moving water
A breeze riffling leaves, skimming the river's skin.

    The nearest put-in a few miles back
        She's traveled a good distance already.

When she dips a cupped hand into the slate river
Throws her head back and lifts the gathered water
    Lets it trickle along her forehead
        Over her eyes and off her chin
She doesn't see me in my lawn chair on the shore
Watching from the shade of a lightning-struck tree.

    With both hands she washes her face
        In the river's cold water
My lips to her forehead, my breath a light breeze
    As she takes up the yellow paddles
        Pushes on under high thin clouds
A range of mountains and cliffs in the distance.

Wolf Moon

Take the clouds, take the snow. Take morning light in a flutter of snowflakes and a winding country road with driveways and mailboxes. Blacktop road, bare trees, three pines side by side sixty feet high, branches loaded with snow. An oak with broken limbs caught in its outstretched arms as if cradling a child. Snowfall. Wind. Man in the road huddled in winter gear, fat leather gloves and black knit hat, long white coat over blue jeans and boots. He's looking down the road where it bends and disappears and a shock of bright sunlight, morning sunlight, the angle low and fierce, lights up the treed hillside, makes it flare amber-gold. Above it a wolf moon in a patch of blue sky. Take a man in the middle of the road, newspaper under his arm, looking up at the white circle of the moon, snowfall and light, as something within him expands until he's no longer there, only moon and light and wind.

Essay: On the Rolling Stones

One more thing I like about the Rolling Stones is that they're still playing.
In the 60s and 70s they were a slap in the face of decorum, kids
With drugs and long hair and ambiguous sexuality, especially Mick
Electric spark of an incandescent being about whom my straight friend
Once said, shocking me: "Dude, I wouldn't throw him out of my bed."
Same with David Bowie though now Bowie's dead and Mick's still here
Climbing to the stage on his seventy-plus-years-old legs: One song
And you see that though the body is ravaged the spirit still rages.

I suppose at some point someone may be reading this after Mick's gone
And I'm gone for that matter, along with everyone else of my generation
Though that doesn't change a thing about this moment, the moment
In which I'm writing this, an icy morning in the mountains of Virginia
February 2016, when Einstein is back in the news with the announcement
That scientists have recorded an audio of two black holes colliding
Which apparently proves a previously unpopular element in his theory
Of relativity, that space and time are connected and changeable.

Not that I have any idea what that means. Or what Einstein meant
When he wrote: "For us physicists, the distinction between past, present
And future is only an illusion, however persistent." Look, I know
Who can you trust if not Albert Einstein, but what can that possibly mean?
Raoul Vezina, Terry Gavin, Jay Walter and Babs. Irving Weiss, Ray Carver
Rick Trethewey, Al Greenberg ... I could go on, adding Einstein himself
Along with my parents and all my aunts and uncles, and all the beautiful
Innocent lost in yet another horror or atrocity: does he mean to say
That they're not truly gone, that they're here with us in the present
That they will be with us in the future and we with them all together
Along with a few hundred billion others, including at some point you
Dear reader? If so that's wonderful though I won't pretend to understand it.
Here for me now in my quiet study the lost are lost and not coming back
Nor can I imagine some way to return to the past for a quick visit

To lay my head on my mother's shoulder or have a talk with my father
Who I'd like to tell I didn't turn out to be quite the screwup he predicted.
And all my lost friends and mentors my teachers and companions—
They all in their bodily presence in their quick lively inventive intelligence
Feel irretrievably lost, my daily life weighted with their silence.

Einstein though, unlike me, is a universally revered genius so maybe he's right
And the poets after all seem mostly to agree with him, from Coleridge to T. S. Eliot—
So sure I'm willing to entertain the possibility: in fact tonight I'll happily, thank you
Go to bed dreaming of a world where Mick goes on prancing up and down the stage
Forever, microphone in hand, and all of us with him in the audience, dancing.